Indonesia

by Robin S. Doak

Content Adviser: Ulrich Kozok,
Assistant Professor, Department of Hawaiian and
Indo-Pacific Languages and Literatures,
University of Hawaii at Manoa

Reading Adviser: Dr. Linda D. Labbo,
Department of Reading Education, College of Education,
The University of Georgia

COMPASS POINT BOOKS
MINNEAPOLIS, MINNESOTA

Compass Point Books
3109 West 50th Street, #115
Minneapolis, MN 55410

Visit Compass Point Books on the Internet at *www.compasspointbooks.com*
or e-mail your request to *custserv@compasspointbooks.com*

On the cover: Dorobudur Monument in Java, Indonesia

Photographs ©: David Samuel Robbins/Corbis, cover; Cory Langley, 4, 34; Wolfgang Kaehler/Corbis, 6–7, 43; Wolfgang Kaehler/www.wkaehlerphoto.com, 8–9, 19, 20, 22, 23, 29, 30, 36, 37, 38, 40; Hulton/Archive by Getty Images, 10, 13, 14, 15, 16; North Wind Picture Archives, 12; Inoong/AFP/ Getty Images, 17; John Elk III, 18, 21, 26, 28, 35, 41; Adek Berry/AFP/Getty Images, 24; Tom Stack & Associates/Gary Milburn, 25; David Ball/Corbis, 27; Simon Bruty/Allsport, 31; Judith Erawati/AFP/ Getty Images, 32; AFP/Corbis, 33; Brand X Pictures, 39; Andy Rain/Getty Images, 42.

Editor: Patricia Stockland
Photo Researcher: Marcie C. Spence
Designer/Page Production: Bradfordesign, Inc./Biner Design
Cartographer: XNR Productions, Inc.

Library of Congress Cataloging-in-Publication Data
Doak, Robin S. (Robin Santos), 1963–
    Indonesia / by Robin S. Doak.
        p. cm. — (First reports)
    Includes index.
    Summary: Introduces the geography, history, culture, and people of Indonesia.
    ISBN 0-7565-0582-8 (hardcover)
    1. Indonesia—Juvenile literature. [1. Indonesia.] I. Title. II. Series.
    DS615.D63 2004
    959.8—dc22   2003014431

Table of Contents

NOTE: In this book, words that are defined in the glossary are
in **bold** the first time they appear in the text.

Selamat datang!

"Selamat datang! Apa kabar?" Welcome! How are you? You might hear these words if you visit the nation of Indonesia. These are phrases in Indonesian, the national language of Indonesia.

Indonesia is the largest nation in Southeast Asia. This big, beautiful country stretches more than 3,200 miles (5,120 kilometers) between the Indian and Pacific

▲ *Welcome to Indonesia!*

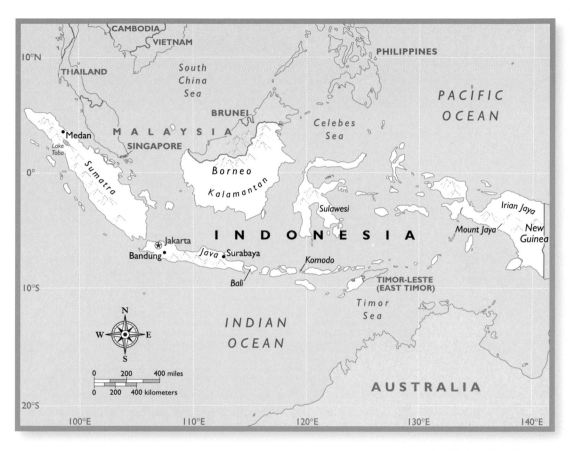

▲ Map of Indonesia

oceans. On the north, Indonesia is bordered by Malaysia, Brunei, the South China Sea, the Celebes Sea, and the Pacific Ocean. On the east, the country is bordered by Papua New Guinea. To the south, the Timor Sea separates Indonesia from Australia. The Indian Ocean is the nation's western boundary.

Land and Weather

Indonesia is the world's largest archipelago. An archipelago is a group of many islands. Indonesia is made up of more than 17,500 islands of many different sizes. People live on about 6,000 of these islands.

Indonesia's five largest islands are Sumatra, Java, Kalimantan (Borneo), Sulawesi, and Irian Jaya. The nation shares the big island of Borneo with Malaysia and Brunei. The island of New Guinea is shared with Papua New Guinea.

▲ *Rice grows well in the hot and humid weather of Indonesia.*

Indonesia is a tropical country. It is located along the **equator.** All year long, temperatures are usually hot and humid. From December to March, Indonesia has a rainy season. Some places get more than 140 inches (356 centimeters) of rain during this period.

Indonesia has many mountains and more than 400 volcanoes. As many as 100 of these volcanoes are still active. Indonesia's highest peak is Mount Jaya on Irian Jaya. It is more than 16,500 feet (5,033 meters) tall. Indonesia also has tropical **rain forests, mangrove swamps,** and sandy beaches.

Indonesia's islands are home to a large variety of big and small animals. These creatures include elephants, tigers, leopards, bears, rhinoceroses, orangutans, wallabies, monkeys, and anteaters. **Cold-blooded** animals found in Indonesia include Komodo dragons, death adders, cobras, and crocodiles. Hundreds of bird species and thousands of types of plants can be found in Indonesia. The nation is famous around the world for its many types of orchids.

▲ *The tiny island of Komodo is home to the Komodo dragon.*
This wild reptile is the largest lizard in the world.

Early History

The ancestors of present-day Indonesians arrived in the archipelago about 4,000 years ago. At first, Indonesia was divided into many tribal societies. Western

▲ *Chinese pepper merchants in Java around 1550 taking part in the spice trade*

Indonesia became involved in the growing international trade of raw materials, goods, and spices about 2,000 years ago. During this time, the tribes established close links with India. Some of them later became kingdoms adopting **Buddhism** and **Hinduism** as their religions.

By the seventh century, three strong kingdoms had taken control of many of the smaller groups. These three kingdoms controlled Indonesia for hundreds of years. During the 1300s and 1400s, Indonesia became known throughout the world as the Spice Islands. Nutmeg, cloves, cinnamon, and other spices grown on the islands were traded to China. Then China sold the goods to Arab traders. By the time the spices reached Europe, they were very expensive.

In the late 1400s, explorers from Europe began to search for the islands. They wanted to control the spice trade. The first Europeans to arrive were

▲ *Dutch ships like these arrived in Indonesia in 1596.*

the Portuguese in 1511. The Portuguese did not treat the native people well, and their rule did not last long.

In 1596, the first Dutch ships arrived in Indonesia. The Dutch seized the important port city of Jakarta on Java. They drove out all other Europeans and began to take control of other islands. The archipelago became a Dutch colony and was known as the Dutch East Indies.

Twentieth Century Indonesia

The people of Indonesia were not happy being ruled by the Dutch. By the early 1900s, many people wanted freedom. Several groups formed to work for Indonesian independence. Millions of Indonesians joined these groups.

During World War II (1939–1945), Japan invaded Indonesia. From 1942 to 1945, Japan controlled the

▲ *Japanese warships off the coast of Indonesia during World War II*

country. Life under the Japanese was harsh. Dutch
people were put into prison camps. Many died.

In August 1945, Japan was defeated in the war.
Indonesian leaders quickly declared that their land
was now free and independent. Although the Dutch

▲ *Indonesian leaders meet to discuss national freedom after World War II.*

▲ *Students in Jakarta speak out in 1965 about changes they want in the government.*

tried once again to take control, their efforts failed. In 1949, they recognized Indonesia as a free nation.

Indonesia's first president was Sukarno. Even now, Sukarno is remembered by Indonesians as a great leader. However, the country remained poor, and many people were starving. In 1965, these conditions led the military to revolt against the government.

General Suharto led a violent takeover, and around 500,000 Indonesians died.

General Suharto took control of the government. Elected president in 1968, Suharto worked to fix Indonesia's struggling economy. Over the next 30 years, he was elected again and again. However, everyone knew that these elections were not fair.

In the 1990s, Indonesia's economy once again began to suffer. Many Indonesians blamed Suharto for these problems. In 1998, he finally resigned as president.

◀ *General Suharto was elected president in 1964.*

In recent years, parts of Indonesia have been rocked by violence and conflict. Some regions are fighting for freedom from the nation. They want to become their own independent nations. In some isolated areas, people of different religions and **cultures** are fighting against one another. Indonesian officials are working to solve these serious problems.

▲ *An Indonesian soldier questions a mother and her children. Some isolated areas are fighting with each other for freedom from the nation.*

The People of Indonesia

▲ *A crowded village in Sumatra*

Indonesia is one of the most heavily populated nations in the world. More than 231 million people live there. That's like squeezing most of the U.S. population into an area that is just three times the size of Texas. While some islands are home to millions of people, others are less crowded. Six out of every 10 Indonesians live in rural areas.

Not all of the people in Indonesia are the same. People from one island may have customs and beliefs that are very different from people on another island. Forty percent of all Indonesians are Javanese, people from the island of Java. There are hundreds of other **ethnic** groups spread throughout the nation.

People in Indonesia speak many different languages. The nation's official language is Indonesian, which is the Indonesian version of the Malay language. Many people also speak Javanese. In addition, there are about 500 other languages used in Indonesia. These languages include Sundanese, many Malay dialects, and Balinese.

▲ *Traditional houses in Sulawesi look like boats.*

Religion in Indonesia

▲ *The Great Mosque in Medan is a place of worship for Muslims.*

Most Indonesians are Muslims, people who follow the teachings of a prophet named Muhammad. Indonesia is home to the world's largest Muslim population. Arab traders brought the Muslim religion to the region in the 12th century. There are many beautiful mosques, or places of worship, throughout the region. Jakarta alone has about 1,000 mosques.

Some of the oldest places of worship in Indonesia are Hindu temples. The Hindu religion came to

Indonesia from India. Most people on the island of Bali are Hindu. Small shrines can be found in homes and other places around the island.

Other people in Indonesia are Christians. **Christianity** was brought to Indonesia by the Dutch. There are both Protestant and Catholic churches throughout the nation.

◀ *The Pura Taman Ayun Temple on Bali, where many people practice Hinduism*

Java

Java is Indonesia's most crowded island. More than half of all Indonesians live there. It is one of the most heavily populated areas in the entire world. There are more than 2,000 people per square mile (2.6 square kilometers) on the island.

▲ *The National Museum in Jakarta is one of many fun places to visit.*

▲ *Jakarta is the largest city in Indonesia.*

Indonesia's three largest cities are located on Java. They are Jakarta, Bandung, and Surabaya. Jakarta is the largest city and the nation's capital. More than 8 million people live there. It is a busy, crowded city.

▲ *Stock traders are a modern part of Indonesia's busy economy.*

Jakarta is the center of Indonesian business and entertainment. Tall, modern office buildings reach high into the sky. For fun, people can visit one of the city's museums or art galleries. They can head to the theater or take part in one of the many festivals held in the city. Jakarta is also a transportation center. Each year, millions of people travel through the city's international airport.

The countryside of Java is famous for its rich, fertile soil. Throughout the island, people make their living growing rice in country villages. Rice terraces on hillsides are a common sight.

▲ *Women harvesting rice on Java*

Other Islands

Sumatra is Indonesia's largest island. It is four times the size of Java, yet fewer people live there. It is a wild, rugged island with many volcanoes. There are also tropical rain forests, sandy beaches, and crystal-clear lakes. Lake Toba on Sumatra is the largest lake in Southeast Asia.

▲ *Lake Toba is located on Sumatra.*

▲ *Tourists can enjoy the Pura Ulan Danu Bratan Temple on Bali.*

Sumatra plays an important role in Indonesia's economy. Many goods are produced on the island. Many more are shipped around the world from Sumatra's largest port in Belawan, a suburb of Medan.

Bali is one of the most popular vacation spots in Indonesia. Each year, millions of tourists come to the

▲ *Warm weather, beautiful plants, and a relaxing atmosphere bring people to Bali.*

small island. They come to see the rich Balinese culture and the beauty of the land with its many volcanoes. They also soak up the sun on Bali's sandy beaches.

One of the wildest areas in Indonesia is Irian Jaya. It makes up the western half of the island of New Guinea. The eastern half is the nation of Papua New Guinea. The jungles of Irian Jaya are still home to tribes that have lived there for thousands of years.

Growing Up in Indonesia

Most students in Indonesia go to public schools. Children begin school when they are 6 years old. They must go to school for nine years. At the age of 15, students can decide whether or not to attend high school. Those who graduate from high school can enroll in one of Indonesia's many universities or colleges.

▲ *A class on Alor Island during a typical school day*

▲ *Girls in Jambaran Bay on Bali dressed in traditional costumes*

People in Indonesia usually dress like people in the United States and other Western countries. A special Indonesian cloth worn by men, women, boys, and girls is the sarong. These wraparound skirts are very popular everywhere in Indonesia.

Like kids all around the world, Indonesian children make time for fun. They may listen to music, play a video game, read a book, or head to the beach. They might also play badminton, soccer, or tennis. These sports are very popular in Indonesia.

▲ *Indonesians enjoy a game of badminton on an outdoor court in Tegal.*

Holidays and Festivals

▲ *During a traditional Galungan ceremony, women bring offerings of fruit and flowers.*

People in Indonesia love to celebrate! Independence Day is held each year on August 17. This national holiday celebrates Indonesia's independence from the Dutch. People in Jakarta have a big parade.

Many other holidays and festivals are held throughout the islands. In Bali, the most important festival is Galungan. It celebrates the victory of good over evil. During Galungan, people on the island hold feasts and decorate temples and shrines.

Idul Fitri is a Muslim holiday that is held throughout Indonesia. The festival marks the end of the Muslim month of fasting. People of all religions join Muslims to celebrate with feasts and firecrackers.

▲ *Chefs build a mosque from chocolate to help celebrate the end of the Muslim month of fasting.*

Funerals are important occasions on many islands. If the dead are not given a proper ceremony, people believe they may cause bad luck for their relatives. Feasts, dancing, and singing help send the dead on their way.

▲ *A beautifully decorated casket is an important part of a funeral on many islands.*

Indonesian Food

▲ *Men sit next to jars of* tuak, *or rice brew.*

Rice is the chief food in Indonesia. It is eaten at breakfast, lunch, and dinner. Rice may be cooked as porridge, fried with meat or vegetables, or eaten with curry or other spicy foods. A popular Indonesian dish is *sate*. It is chunks of chicken or goat meat roasted on a skewer and some-times served with peanut sauce. Another Indonesian favorite is *krupuk*, which is fish- or shrimp-flavored chips.

One unique Indonesian dish is *tempe*. It is a cake made of fermented soybeans. The food, first created in Java, is popular with vegetarians everywhere. Tempe is usually fried and seasoned with spices before being served.

For dessert, Indonesia offers a wide variety of tropical fruits. These include pineapple, guava, mango, papaya, and star fruit.

▲ *Local fruits make delicious desserts.*

Arts and Music

▲ *At a batik factory, a woman applies wax to fabric.
This will leave decorative patterns after it is dyed.*

Indonesia has a rich history of art, music, and dance.
Batik is one colorful craft that had its start in Indonesia.
Batik is a design on cloth that is created with wax
and dye.

▲ *A gamelan orchestra*

Gamelan is a type of Indonesian music. Gamelan orchestras include gongs, drums, bamboo flutes, and xylophones. This music has been played on the islands for many centuries.

Dancing is an important part of Indonesian life. People dance at weddings, funerals, feasts, and other important occasions. Some of the most famous dances are Balinese temple dances. Temple dancers dress in fancy, colorful costumes. Some dancers wear masks. The slow, graceful dances often tell a story.

▲ *A masked Balinese temple dancer*

Wayang, or shadow puppet plays, are very popular in Indonesia. During a play, a puppeteer may control as many as 50 different puppets. Many of the plays tell ancient stories and myths that have been passed down through the ages. Others may teach lessons on how to behave properly.

◄ *Wayang golek puppets, used to tell stories and myths, are very popular in Indonesia.*

Indonesia Today

▲ *In Kalibukbuk on Bali, a farmer plows a rice field.*

Indonesia has a wealth of natural resources. Ash from the many volcanoes has made the soil rich and good for farming. The top crops in Indonesia include rice, rubber, palm oil, coffee, tea, and cocoa.

▲ *A man gathers sulphur from Mount Ijen. Sulphur is one of many natural resources in Indonesia.*

Many metals and minerals are found in Indonesia. Tin, nickel, copper, coal, gold, and silver are all mined here. Oil and natural gas also can be found.

Workers in Indonesia make many types of goods and products. Textiles, coffee, clothes, shoes, cement, and chemicals are just a few of the items made on the islands. Indonesian goods are shipped and sold all over the world.

Some of Indonesia's businesses have hurt the land. Forests have been destroyed for timber, and factories have polluted air and water. Many islands that make up Indonesia disagree on economic and political issues. The nation continues to work to improve these conditions. With its exciting blend of people, cultures, and places, Indonesia has a strong future.

▲ *Women weave colorful textiles in a factory on Sumatra.*

Glossary

Buddhism—an Eastern religion that follows the teachings of Gautama Buddha

Christianity—the faith that believes Jesus Christ is the Son of God

cold-blooded—an animal whose body temperature changes as its environment changes

cultures—groups of people who share beliefs, customs, and a way of life

ethnic—relating to a culture or nationality

equator—an imaginary line around the middle of Earth

Hinduism—an Eastern religion practiced widely throughout India having many gods and goddesses

mangrove swamps—low-lying, marshy wetlands with tropical trees and shrubs that have many prop roots

rain forests—a dense tropical forest where a lot of rain falls

Did You Know?

- In 1890, scientists discovered the bones of a prehistoric man on the island of Java. "Java Man" proves that people lived in Indonesia nearly 2 million years ago.

- The orangutan is found only in Indonesia. These big, orange apes live in the hot forests of Sumatra and Kalimantan.

- Indonesia often suffers from earthquakes and volcanic eruptions. In 1883, Krakatoa volcano, between Java and Sumatra, erupted. The explosion was one of the largest ever recorded on Earth.

Official name: Republik Indonesia
(Republic of Indonesia)

Capital: Jakarta

Official language: Indonesian (Bahasa Indonesia)

National song: Indonesia Raya ("Great Indonesia")

Area: 741,099 square miles (1,926,857 square kilometers)

Highest point: Mount Jaya, 16,500 feet (5,033 meters) above sea level (Mandala Peak)

Lowest point: Sea level

Population: 231,328,092 (2002 estimate)

Head of government: President

Money: Rupiah

Important Dates

10–499	Indonesia becomes involved in international trade, especially with India and China.
1596	The first Dutch ships arrive in Indonesia. Over the next 300 years, the Dutch control the region.
1883	Krakatoa volcano erupts, creating one of the largest explosions in history.
1890	Scientists discover "Java Man."
1942	Japan invades Indonesia during World War II.
1945	Sukarno declares Indonesia an independent nation on August 17.
1949	The Dutch recognize Indonesia as an independent nation on December 27.
1965	Sukarno's government is overthrown by General Suharto; hundreds of thousands of Indonesians die in the violence.
1968	Suharto becomes Indonesia's second president on March 27.
1998	Suharto resigns as president after Indonesia's economy collapses.

Want to Know More?

At the Library

Fisher, Frederick. *Indonesia*. Milwaukee, Wis.: Gareth Stevens, 2000.

Furgang, Kathy. *Krakatoa: History's Loudest Volcano*. New York: Powerkids Press, 2001.

Mirpouri, Gouri. *Indonesia*. New York: Tarrytown, 2002.

On the Web

For more information on Indonesia, use FactHound to track down Web sites related to this book.

1. Go to *www.compasspointbooks.com/facthound*
2. Type in this book ID: 0756505828
3. Click on the *Fetch It* button.

Your trusty FactHound will fetch the best Web sites for you!

On the Road

The United States-Indonesia Society

1625 Massachusetts Ave. N.W., Suite 550

Washington, DC 20036-2260

202/232-1400

usindo@usindo.org

To learn more about the relationship between Indonesia and the United States

Through the Mail

Embassy of the Republic of Indonesia

2020 Massachusetts Ave.

Washington, DC 20036

For more information on the culture of Indonesia

Index

About the Author

Robin S. Doak has been writing for children for more than 14 years. A former editor of Weekly Reader and U*S*Kids magazine, Ms. Doak has authored fun and educational materials for kids of all ages. Some of her work includes biographies of explorers such as Henry Hudson and John Smith, as well as other titles in this series. Ms. Doak is a past winner of the Educational Press Association of America Distinguished Achievement Award. She lives with her husband and three children in central Connecticut.